Detours

Aymeric Fromentin

BookLeaf Publishing

Presentation by *BookLeaf Publishing*

Web: www.bookleafpub.com

E-mail: info@bookleafpub.com

ISBN: 9789357696678

First edition 2023

DEDICATION

This book is dedicated to the moments that are part of our daily lives but never make it into our daily discussions. The moments that bind us together yet remain unspoken of. To the marvel, grandeur, amazement, and wonderful that keep the fabric of our lives together.

Stories

There are stories behind every word, every whisper, behind every blink and every smile. Stories behind every one too many drinks, every missed phone call, every unanswered letter and every late night out.

Stories that are told, stories that are painted, stories that are screamed and stories that are quietened. Stories that should be known, stories that should be forgotten, stories that should be remembered and stories that should be invented.

For people are real, people are unique, people are there and people are all the same. They are young, bold, committed, soulful, original, striving, afraid, tired, on a quest, full of hope, disoriented, wondering, handsome, crazy, creative, plain, they are right, they are wrong, they look for something to live for and find something to die for, and sometimes it is the contrary, and sometimes it is the same old story, they love the sun, they love the night, they fall sick in the heat and are scared of the dark, people are old, weary, and jaded and they die.

There's a story behind each person behind each story of each person in this infinite story of time and places. For what is this reality but a story told with sounds and images, with shapes and vibrations, colours and riddles always twisting, entangling and coming back to the neverending stage of life?

And I can't help but wonder, who's the audience of this narrative roulette? For whom does the curtain raise, for whose sport do we live, hope, despair and die, who laughs at these illusions, these sights, these dreams and these lies?

Please, come here, sit a moment, look up to the sky, enjoy the silence, here you will find the splinters, fragments, and fractals of these moments all lost in the spiral of time. And please be careful not to lose your way, lest you may find yourself in here as well. You wouldn't want that to happen, would you?

Well, would you?

It is an amiss sensation

It has been going on in your mind for days on end, singing colours have been forming the tempo of your inner voice, waves crashing on the shore of your mind's eye that you're dying to turn into lines and verses. And when you sit with your manuscript, when you sit with your lover, when the world is listening…
Void. Silence. It is all gone. The words won't materialise. As if there were not enough of them in all the languages known to Humankind. The brutal realisation comes to you that what you feel here and now can never be expressed. As if circumstances like yours were never meant to be taken into account. It is an amiss sensation, that you are the first to ever go through such a rabbit hole of memories and feelings and abstractions. And you wonder, did you not learn the words or did the language never learn you? Perhaps it is all the books, perhaps you did not read enough of them, or perhaps your mind was not sharp enough to let you craft your speech as masters do. That feeling in your gut that your voice is not meant to be heard, perhaps you should have trusted it after all.
Or perhaps, perhaps we need more words.
After all, your life is the only version of the human experience as you are living it now that will ever exist. It is priceless. It's for that kind of odyssey that new words need to be invented, and maybe your life will be lived to the fullest once you will have added to the

human lexicon the words that crystallise the uniqueness
of what you saw, what you felt, what you were.
And what no tongue nor speech nor term can ever set in
stone what is given for you and you alone to treasure.

Bad weather

Language commits the capital crime of cursing the weather whenever it wards us off from gallivanting in the great outdoors. Bad weather, miserable sky, insufferable conditions, will the slander ever stop? My eyes water at such beauty as the rain. My ears whistle with the swoosh of the wind. Rugged weather in all its bearings boasts a beauty that knows no bound. Nothing feels more alive than a thunderstorm above an unleashed ocean, nothing is worthier of a painting than snowfall under the northern lights.

The rain is my blessing. It protects me.

It stops humans from expecting my presence in the outside world, it quells the pressure to hike or swim or shop or tan or pose for pictures in searing sunlight. I say, deliver me from beach weather and tan sessions. I say, shield me from big days out and peer pressure. Give me the smell of brewing coffee by the fireplace, give me a whole day to read and write while the raindrops stream down my window, give me a rumbling night sky while I drift to sleep under a double quilt. Let me forget the chaos and rumble before I lose sight of myself.

I know why after a gentle drizzle, plants smell like bliss.

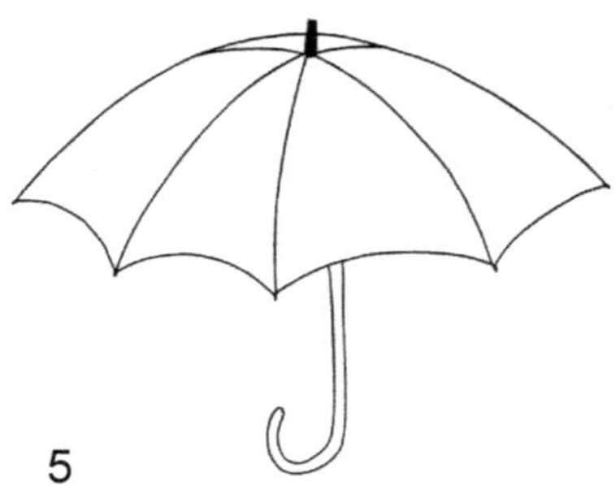

We gift kids trampolines

We gift kids trampolines so they learn how to bounce,
the one skill that proves most decisive in adult life.
Bounce from degrees to jobs to relationships to bills
to insurance to heartbreak to pills to social media to
improv classes to online dating to failed dreams to
nothing. Kids will not remember much of this
moment in the future.
What grown-ups love to remember is every bump on
the road, every wrong turn taken, every fork in the
path that we decided not to take only so we could
convince ourselves we should have gone the other
way. The mind loves nothing more than a failed past.
The tragedy is, there's no stopping ourselves from
fabricating an infinite supply of it. The difference
between a child and an adult is how long the list of
regrets goes.
A trampoline, a summer day, hot cheeks, a laugh,
that's what they will carry away and cherish,
forgetful of the year, the names, the clouds. You too
know them, the blurry memories that feel like home,
that you can't put a date on or a place or a time or if
they are real or dreamt yet they will forever define
joy to you, the days before lessons, the life before
life, the bliss before decisions.

Limbs like cotton

Limbs like cotton, head like a biscuit dunked in a glass of wine by a housewife in denial, the only regular heartbeat is that of the clock, stringing out the moments of your life second after second after second. You are past counting how many hours you spent waking too much, sleeping too little. Yet you can't stop. You have to stay awake, you have to steal some out-of-schedule time, you have to reclaim control of your life, you have to manifest that no matter the shift, the homework, the family picnics, or the healthy lifestyle gurus, you are still in control of your life, and you will indulge in your passions at the hour when only sinners are awake. You will read the next chapter, you will write another page, you will shade the illustration, you will keep the story going. And when you stretch and knead your eyelids, your tendon as creaky as the chair you sit on, you raise your eyes to your dormer and that's when, in the blue and black blend of sapphire sky and Indian ink earth, you notice them. Tiny islets of light, scattered here and there, introverted windows hanging by themselves in the night like the wallflowers of sleep, like the portholes of spaceships drifting in space. You raise your eyes and you see me and I see you, and I know why you are awake, and I share in your quest for truth at a time when no one can tell us off, and I know who you are, and you know who I am, for at

that moment, united in transgression, we share the
will to escape, to forget, to conquer, to assert, to dare,
to learn, to dream awake. We know our favourite
works were not written in the daytime.

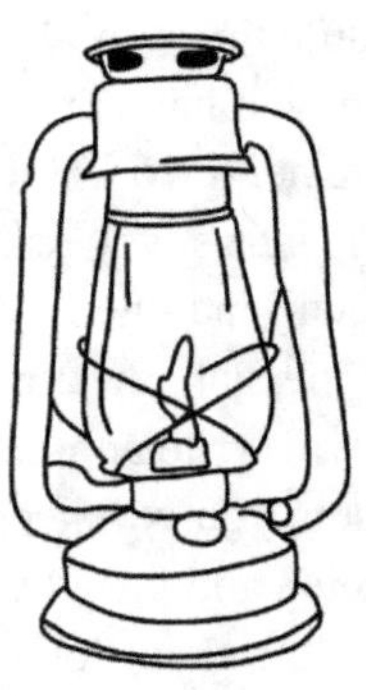

I wonder if café owners know

I wonder if café owners know their business is not to sell coffee. It is to give people a space where they can take shelter from the rain, observe other humans, have their first and last dates, use the bathroom when they leave home too fast, and take out a notebook to pretend they are writers.

Seasons

When flowers shine and perfumes exhume
I felt her heart beat in the palm of my hand
High was the sun and warm was the sand
When we fell in love in the season of bloom.

Remember aeons when we knew how to fly
Such a spell possessed me when together we danced
What force is summoned when the soul is entranced?
We shared an embrace in the season of sky.

Yet as our union only grazed adolescence
Dark ailments befell her and drained her essence
She turned cold and dead in the season of pale light.

Nothing left to touch but a void in the air
Nothing left to hear but echoes of despair
I became mad in the season of white.

Every child's bedroom

You see it in every child's bedroom, a mount of fluffies so warm and fuzzy you wish you could hug them all at once. Yet you know, because the child you were once knows, that amongst them is a fluffy that sits at a special place in a child's heart. One comfort toy the child will always grab to fall asleep, that the child turns to for protection, reassurance, for peace of mind. One that the young mind will unfailingly choose, a forever companion. A talisman.
We are no children anymore, yet we kept this habit going, you and me, after all this time. We have access, at the tip of our touch, to every piece of art ever created, stored in the ether of the great digital archive. All the more so strange is this impulse to go back to the same works we already know by heart. Films we quote, songs we sing along to, and books we read so many times we feel related to the author. They feel like home. These talismans. You need them to cheer you up, to remind you of what matters, to ward off evil thoughts, and to connect with those you love. Some works, you know you'll never stop coming back to them. You may even feel pangs of shame now and then when you think of all the time spent going over works you are already familiar with, but that will never dim the joy of reuniting with those old friends. We need not always turn to art for challenge and provocation. Sometimes art is only

meant to bring us solace like this soft fluffy we used
to hug to sleep.

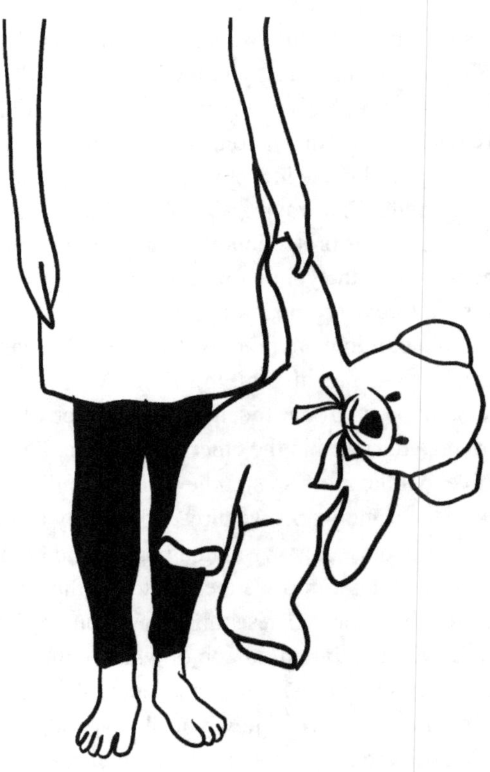

The train home

If you have ever ridden the metro home at night after an endless work shift, you know that joy is forever banned from those grounds. People hardly bother to show any sign of life anymore, their minds already withdrawn far away, even colours seem to have left their faces. United in indifference, you share this moment altogether, yet you can't feel connected to these silhouettes. You can't because in your hands, from dunes of paper and ink, characters spring alive and guide you to other times, other places, to the peaks and valleys of their arcs and narratives, and you feel reality bend around you. For in a moment, in a few lines on a dog-eared page, a character puts into a few words thoughts and feelings you have struggled to express for years without knowing how to. And the world fades around you, your mind's eye is wide open, and you feel more akin to archetypes and plot devices than you will ever be to your fellow human beings. A strange nostalgia fills you, a dread that no one will ever understand you as well as a character who only exists with a lifespan of three hundred pages. Fiction makes it so pleasing to be estranged from reality. The tragedy is how we forget someone just like us gave a voice to the protagonists we cherish, how the clarity of thought, the sum of adventures, and the soft warm words were written by someone just like us, who might have lived far away long ago, or who might be very much alive still, whom we could meet, who could be on the train here with us, who could be us. Could be you. Regardless of how diluted it is when it reaches the audience, entertainment is always someone's life story at the start.

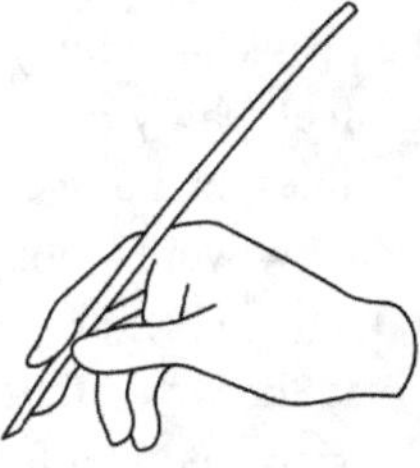

I'm scared of time travel

I'm scared of time travel. I'm scared of how fast it happens to me. There's no controlling it. Anything can be the trigger, a sight, a sound, a scent, and I blink out of the present. Not there anymore. Before I know it, life dissolves in a watercolour of days bygone, inhabited by faces whose names are lost to time, snippets of life kids today would not understand.

Construction sites and their vapours of solvent, a summer sunset that tastes like cherries, a teddy bear that sits quietly on a freshly made bed, these are all as many time portals that wind life some decades back.

It's a curious trick of the mind to sprinkle the world of anchor points onto which it will forever latch no matter how far away you have stridden as if it knew it would need emergency exits for when reality becomes too unseemly to see, too heavy to heave. Connections our young neurons weaved between memories and stimuli, before they turned jaded by a routine they hardly bother to imprint anymore.

You know what I am referring to.

The Land of Ever-Joy

All gents and lassies from near and afar,
All gather and shine in joy and delight.
People in this land all smile under the star
For they know, anytime, may burn out their light.

You may well rather smile and forget all tears
When air carries metal and blood strikes stone.
Just pretend life is only joys and no fears
When all you can do is carve your tombstone.

Did the fools know, did they also smile,
When the symbols of power, they forged in fire,
Did they know of the dreaded price of their guile,
Of all them of their kind that would join the pyre?

And all people smile from even to morn
In that land of grey where all sorrows are born.

Home

Home is the sound of a lock that bolts shut and echoes softly in the corridor. The sound that puts up a wall between you and the outside world, the sound that means no one can get to you for the rest of the day, that you are free to indulge in what makes your soul shine. Home is the path you stumble along in the morning when you are still drowsy. It is the familiar tick of a clock, it is the smell of freshly dried clothes, it is the reflection of sunlight in the water of a flower vase. Home is the sanctum only the closest ones will ever be invited to enter. It is a place no amount of money or power or negotiation can force open. Your personality, your memories show in the pictures on the wall, in the colours of the curtains, in every trinket on the tables and in every book on your bedside.

No matter your age, your station in life, or the amount of money in your account, home is forever a myriad of tiny heartfelt details. It is where you wake up every morning, cook for your loved ones, the place you tidy up with affection, where you are not afraid to laugh and cry, where you don't need to pretend.

Home is the ones you share it all with.

It means you are safe.

It means you made it.

No matter the places you move to,

you will always come home.

The Lightweaver and the Streamsinger

In another land, under another sky,
The winds tell a story, on and on, as they fly.
A legend sure it is, just a bedtime story,
For children dreamy, and adults lonely.
Under a white sun, as the earth blackens,
Wanderers will sing it to whoever listens,
And as Time passes, ever more so jaded,
So came and went the two who never were united.
I beg thee come close now, and if some time you will spare me,
Of he the light and she the sea, the tale I shall tell thee.
There is a kin to whom the sky is more than blue and air,
T'is a canvas to paint on, with lights and colours fair.
As feathers and leaves, they soar, stars and clouds are their friends,
When they touch our earthly shore, all our ailments they cleanse.
Their fingers are like pencils, of sunlight they make their ink,
A wave of their hand draws masterpieces in the time we need to
blink.
Then there are others, from the deep and dark they arise
And by the sound of their voice make the oceans wake and rise.
The depths are their kingdom, sea currents they ride,
When our earthly shore they touch, our whole world must abide.
The waves are their verses, the rivers their chorus,
Their lullabies are streams and tsunamis their arias.
Thus are the spirits and sprites that make our world go round
Lightweavers and Streamsingers are the names by which they're
known.

Faraway land of myths and wonders, in there once upon a time
A foolish one and a soulful other tangled in an unlikely rhyme.
A Lightweaver from the sky was he in all aspects
Drawing and painting on starshine and sunbeams,
A Streamsinger from the sea was she in all respects
Chanting and singing to rivers and sea streams.
As surely as the day shall never meet the night
The two tribes were bound to never share flight.
Yet in dusk and dawn, where liminal they linger
Stars were crossed and doom stroke, the impossible did occur.
It was so that every evening and every morning,
Waves came crashing against coasts of stone, foaming.
Lights of fire hovered over dark waters
Shadows roamed amidst shipwrecks and anchors.
Every time he from the skies beheld the sea and marvelled,
Every time she from the sea stared at the skies and yearned.
The heavens looked ever so lifting, the abyss ever so deep.
And always they would both dream of them in their sleep.
When they woke, they'd drift evermore closer to the surface,
That fragile mirror of water and air which remained ever still and
seamless.
Him weaving lights into wisps o'the will
Her singing streams what destiny they had to fulfil.
As they got closer, they noticed each other,
Their fingertips grazed, they looked deep into each other,
Their breaths became one in a second that lasted forever.
And in that fateful moment, all began and was over.
The globe turned and night and day
In separate hemispheres each other gave way.
Lightweaver, Streamsinger, alone again they were,
Of a strange warmth and emptiness, they could feel the flutter.
High in the sky, he bore with him a dear memory

Of a voice that made water run with peace or fury
Deep under the sea, she dreamt about the sight
Of fiery hands that shaped colours and light.
They knew they could never meet, lest day and night conjointly happened,
Yet inside their heart, a longing for dusk and dawn was quickened.
They felt a new force run through their being,
The echo of a pure, unaltered feeling,
A connection stronger than with any other creature living,
And through day and night, through sun and storm, they waited, yearning.
They waited, for every time they saw each other,
The light in myriads of fractals exploded over the azure,
The seas rose turquoise and the rivers gleamed,
The dolphins danced on waves undreamed.
Transcended they were, her voice became strongest,
She made the seas of the world go round in wanderlust,
And his auroras turned the skies into a painting in motion,
Charging each sunset and daybreak with vibrant emotion.
When they touch flames rose all over the horizon,
And a pure song echoed in all the whirlpools of the ocean.
But as the fleeting moments of their meeting grew ever more passionate
Days and nights became bleaker at an equal rate.
As in those periods, waiting, they now went inanimate,
Their beauty was never to be seen by sun or moon
Climates went dull and the seasons were out of tune,
Lightweavers and Streamsingers peoples became, slowly, desperate.
For theirs was the mission to keep the wheel of cosmos turning,
And the love their children shared left it in chaos sinking.
One day in the North and night in the South,

Or maybe that was the other way around,
The enticed two were in reverie lost when the elders came forth
To make them see the truth of the world they were running aground.
They were first dumbfounded, what they were told they could not hear,
Argued it was not for two poor souls to fracture the celestial sphere,
Then felt anger and rage ignite in their chests,
As if their kin were playing on them the cruellest jests,
Invoking a time-forsaken law of Nature to dismiss
The bond that united them, that, for all they saw, was crystalised bliss.
Passions ran high, and the eldest had not decoded
The gifts this obsession upon the young souls had bestowed.
Their powers were now beyond reach and none could tame
The wild beasts that the lovers in a heartbeat became.
The watery halls trembled of a roar till then never heard
And air and clouds and stars dissolved as the sky itself ruptured.
Their auras amplified, wide, wide, until the oceans' surface was punctured,
Until all of Nature was almost disordered.
There they saw each other, in their horror and glory,
Their beauty vanished, their traits deformed by fury.
As all collided a voice without age and place
Spoke to their minds and in them left its trace.
The voice of the void with timeless wisdom said
There was a way to stop that mad dread,
They would have to pay a dear price, however,
One of them had to leave all behind
And rejoin the other in the world of the other kind,
He had to become Streamsinger, or her, Lightweaver.

So said the voice then forever disappeared
Leaving the two creatures, hearts lost, minds bleared.
Silence was. Then denial. Then bargain. Then anger again.
They wanted to plea, they wished for the voice to hear their pain,
The voice or anyone else who had the power to revert their fate,
But they knew there was no other way. Of their plight, they felt the
weight.
Slowly their auras regressed, obscurity fell,
They lost sight of each other and it resounded of farewell.
The dawn that came then, the sunset that came after,
Were bleak and sad, lifeless, without their ardour.
They remained alone and pondered
Over the frailty of life and its quest for sense left unanswered.
Deep inside, a truth more unbearable even,
Than the truth by the voice of the void spoken
He contemplated light weave, she listened to streams sing,
The truth of their hearts was relentless, unyielding,
Deeply in love they were, of this there was no doubt,
But sacrificing all they were, that, they could not,
For they knew, should they abandon,
The lights, the oceans, no victory would be won,
It would sadden them forever, and of love, there would be left
none.
No word ever voiced the dreadful decision
Only their minds were clear on what needed be done,
They couldn't be together, or all there was would burn,
They couldn't be someone else, lest what they'd be they'd spurn.
From that dark moment on, and ever, each other they shun.
He rose high in the sky, higher than any before,
And the blue of the ocean he ever saw no more.
She dived deep into the abyss, till she could touch the globe's core,
And there she stayed and sang, never again to see the shore.

For ages past this story, the world remained a dismal place,
Until in time it recovered, seasons regained their pace.
Beauty and soul returned, day by day, year by year,
Now just the poets will tell this sad story of love sincere.
The marvels of Nature we still can admire,
From emerald northern lights to seas of sapphire,
And if you come one day alone, to admire daybreak or sunset,
And your thoughts start drifting as if by feelings beset,
Now you know of a tale that will echo forever and ever,
The legend of the Lightweaver and the Streamsinger.

Remember

Remember, when you touch a book, it is not only ink and paper you skim. It is someone's insomnia, doubt, madness, and perhaps masochism. Hope. Words that torture a writer, need to be told, crave to be heard, and maybe, the promise of making the sun shine a little bit brighter.

Prayer

They flock by the billions
Join hands
Fall to their knees
Whisper to the unseen
They claim the other world
For themselves
So they may grovel
For more wealth
Fewer sorrows
And to defer
The awakening
Of death
A little longer.
Perhaps they hope
To change
What comes after.
They won't.

Words of envy
Words of greed
Words of folly
Words of nothing

Pray for fair winds
And clear water
For merciful weather
And distinct seasons
Pray the trees bear fruits

And the earth grows plants
Pray dissension ends
And life heals
The gain of one
Is the loss of another
And the pain of one
Is the pain of all.

Pray not for you
Pray for all
Pray you are not alone.
Pray for the wisdom
To know not to pray
Pray for the fortitude
To never want to pray.

So many times

I woke up so many times to the same day I don't remember
if I'm awake or asleep.
You're the push of a button away yet I can't take that leap.
I already did. I already skid.
Now I make rhymes of the same chord like a broken record.
All that remains is for the rain to wash away the stains.
I try to forget, shake myself and make do
But everywhere I glance reality looks like you.

The truth of the cosmos

The truth of the cosmos
Lies beyond our grasp
On a scale where we hardly began
And already ended
Forever out of reach
Forever out of sight
Never meant for us to behold
The miracle of this creation
The undying dance
Of light and space
Of stars and planets
We are but a flicker
A remnant of the first blast
A ripple soon to vanish
Life is a chance occurrence
An unforeseen consequence
Of the spark that started
The celestial swirl's waves
We will never be granted
Its contemplation
Nor its comprehension
Such is Creation's curse
The final mystery
Never to be solved
Gift me a summer night

And a timeless desert
So I can lie between worlds
And fall into the sky
Let me see the pulsars burn
And the stars ignite
Bathe me in stardust
Let my eyes gaze
In the astral void
Upon the light of dead suns
To forget the agony
Of the planet I die on

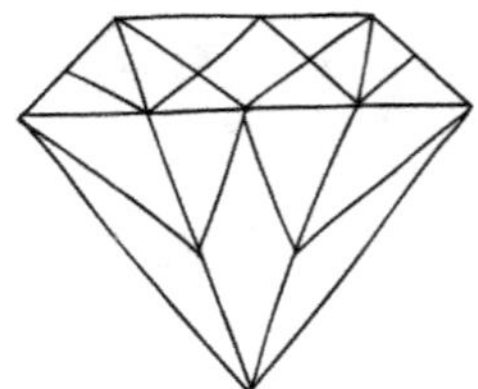

How lucky I got

I couldn't believe how lucky I got when our paths collided. They were not supposed to. Maybe that was the problem. You bid me farewell when you realised you'd rather marry someone more like you. I don't blame you. I'd rather marry someone like you too.

Scene

Action.

We like to believe we are the hero of the story. The limelight is on us, it has to be. From birth and growth, trials and losses, we learned our lessons, and accepted the sacrifices.
Plot twists, chance meetings, last-minute saves, there are too many of them for it to be random luck. Above all, too many tragedies. Life is in no way realistic. Life is a film written to make the audience laugh a little and cry a lot, and all of us have been cast to be its protagonist. One long sequence shot filmed exclusively through our eyes. Unedited, uncensored, director's cut. We even root for ourselves, eager to hit the big reveal, the apotheosis, the resurrection moment when we turn into who we are.
And yet.
And yet sometimes, when the plot falls flat, when the script shows no lines, the feeling downs on us. The feeling that perhaps we did not land the leading role. Days blur into one another in a long succession of cutaways as if our part was left out of the master cut. The slithering silhouette of suspicion slides into our spirit, susurrating how we might have been a secondary character, or tertiary, or a placeholder, and what little part we had is already played out, and while the twists and turns continue for the main

character, we are left hoping extras are also allowed
some measure of closure sometimes.
Yet that's not the worst.
The worst is when you understand you were the bad
guy all along.

And cut.

Midnight poem

Write a poem in the middle of the night because you
procrastined all day.
Write a poem with your heart and soul when all your
heart and soul want is to get done with it so you can
go to bed.
Want to know how to do it?
Begin by addressing the reader directly to challenge
them to continue reading.
Make it fierce.
Make it true.
Make a clean break with all the rules and metrics and
stylistic devices that you are too impatient to follow
anyway, just write whatever comes to mind in one
long stream of consciousness, you know some will
read it as a bold statement of ownership and a new
definition of a venerable genre. Throw in some
beloved postmodern quirks like self-awareness,
metatextuality, and quotable content. Now you just
need to play with the form of your manuscript with
Lines
Of
A
Single
Word
~~And some crossed-out verse~~
Now bring it all to an end with an observation of the
futile yet redeeming nature of art in the face of the
fragile randomness of life.

You can maybe add a rhyme or two
Should you feel like it was all too easy
Yet pentameters do feel odd to you
Classic lit makes you feel all dizzy.
Of this strange draft, we now reach the end
I hope you enjoyed my scribbles
The essence of writing I strive to transcend
And in these lands, I wish you safe travels.

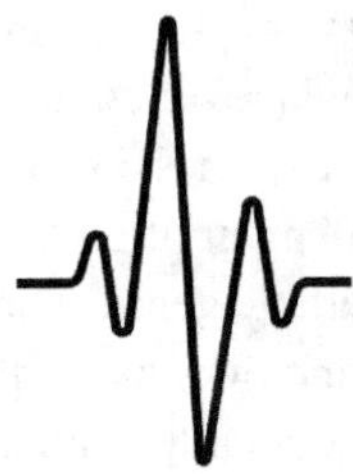

I'll tell you a story

I'll tell you a story. There are eight billion characters
in it.
In this chapter they're all connected to one another.
It's making nothing easier.
The more they speak the less they hear.
They can't say what it is they are after
But it sure is killing the planet
They only disagree on how to do it.
Somehow they all believe they are the good guy
They all have a perfect plan in mind
And they never seem to know how to put it into
motion
Random incidents have more impact on their life
Than carefully planned and prepared actions.
You have to wonder really, when you watch them toil
How much do they decide, and how much is sheer
luck
How real free will is, I wonder sometimes,
When it is stated in eight billion paradigms.
I often stop to ask myself
Were we happier when it was all simpler?
When the world was smaller
And there were fewer choices.
Was it easier to know the way ahead?
To make it all work?
Maybe it was not meant to become that complex.
Maybe. Maybe not.
Maybe the whole point of this world being made

Was simply for it to be tossed around
Like a little blue ball
Thrown for the sport of faceless giants.
I'll tell you a story and I'll take my leave.
There are eight billion characters and no one
remembers how they got into it.

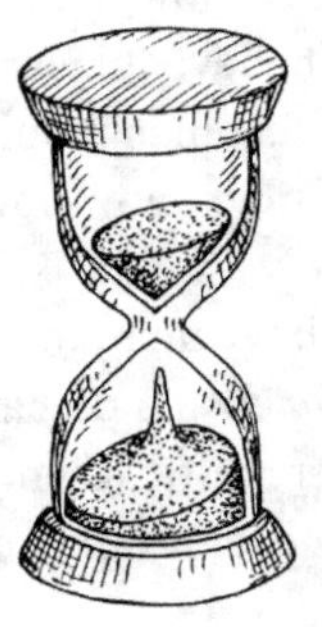